But This War
Had Such Promise

Doonesbury books by G. B. Trudeau

Still a Few Bugs in the System
The President Is a Lot Smarter Than You Think
But This War Had Such Promise
Call Me When You Find America
Guilty, Guilty, Guilty!
"What Do We Have for the Witnesses, Johnnie?"
Dare To Be Great, Ms. Caucus
Wouldn't a Gremlin Have Been More Sensible?
"Speaking of Inalienable Rights, Amy . . ."
You're Never Too Old for Nuts and Berries
An Especially Tricky People
As the Kid Goes for Broke
Stalking the Perfect Tan
"Any Grooming Hints for Your Fans, Rollie?"
But the Pension Fund Was Just Sitting There
We're Not Out of the Woods Yet
A Tad Overweight, but Violet Eyes to Die For

In Large Format

The Doonesbury Chronicles
Doonesbury's Greatest Hits

a Doonesbury classic by

G B Trudeau.

But This War Had Such Promise

Holt, Rinehart and Winston
New York

Published by Holt, Rinehart and Winston, 383 Madison Avenue,
New York, New York 10017.

Published simultaneously in Canada by Holt, Rinehart and
Winston of Canada, Limited.

Library of Congress Catalog Card Number: 72-91561

ISBN: 0-03-007521-1

Printed in the United States of America

The cartoons in this book have appeared in newspapers
in the United States and abroad under the auspices of
Universal Press Syndicate.

10 9

GBTrudeau

MOTHER?... HI. SON MICHAEL HERE.

LISTEN, MOM, I'VE GOT SOME NEWS. I'M START- ING A COMMUNE WITH A BUNCH OF FRIENDS. THIS WEEK. MARK IS WORKING OUT THE LEASE AR- RANGEMENTS FOR A HOUSE IN THE COUNTRY.

NOW, MOM, BEFORE YOU GET UPSET, LET ME EXPLAIN. I... WHAT, MOM?...

SHE WANTS TO JOIN US.

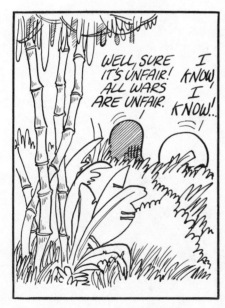